D1609420

CHALLENGES FOR DEMOCRACY

Media Literacy: Information and Disinformation

Kathryn Hulick

ReferencePoint Press®

San Diego, CA

About the Author

Kathryn Hulick is the author of numerous books for young readers. Her book Welcome to the Future (Quarto, 2021) explores how technology may transform the world in the future. She is also a contributing editor at *Muse* magazine and writes news and features for Science News for Students and Front Vision, a Chinese-language science magazine. She enjoys hiking, painting, reading, and working in her garden. She lives in Massachusetts with her husband, son, and dog.

For more information, contact:
ReferencePoint Press, Inc.
PO Box 27779
San Diego, CA 92198
www.ReferencePointPress.com

Picture Credits:

Cover: Andrey Burmakin/Shutterstock.com
    Easycamera/Shutterstock.com
    Tero Vesalainen/Shutterstock.com

4: Maury Aaseng
6: lev radin/Shutterstock.com
10: David J. Martin/Shutterstock.com
14: fizkes/Shuttterstock.com
19: diy13/Shuttestock.com
20: a katz/Shutterstock.com

24: Associated Press
30: Bridgeman Images
32: Associated Press
34: Maury Aaseng
38: Eman Kazemi/Alamy Stock Photo
41: pruciatti/iStock
43: DenPhotos/Shutterstock.com
47: Vitalii Stock/Shutterstock.com
50: DenPhotos/Shutterstock.com
53: Insta_photos/Shutterstock.com

LIBRARY OF CONGRESS CATALOGING-IN-PUBLICATION DATA

Names: Hulick, Kathryn, author.
Title: Media literacy : information and disinformation / by Kathryn Hulick.
Description: San Diego : ReferencePoint Press, 2022. | Series: Challenges
  for democracy | Includes bibliographical references and index.
Identifiers: LCCN 2021056550 (print) | LCCN 2021056551 (ebook) | ISBN
  9781678203047 (library binding) | ISBN 9781678203054 (ebook)
Subjects: LCSH: Media literacy--Juvenile literature.
Classification: LCC P96.M4 H85 2022 (print) | LCC P96.M4 (ebook) | DDC
  302.23--dc23/eng/20211220
LC record available at https://lccn.loc.gov/2021056550
LC ebook record available at https://lccn.loc.gov/2021056551

CONTENTS

Young Americans Have Low Opinion of US Democracy

American democracy has been experiencing many challenges. Foremost among those challenges is the widespread perception that US democracy is either "in trouble" or "failing." This is the view of a majority of young Americans, age eighteen to twenty-nine. A national poll conducted in Fall 2021 by the Harvard Kennedy School Institute of Politics finds that only 7 percent of young adults view the United States as a "healthy democracy."

Which of the following phrases best describes the United States today?

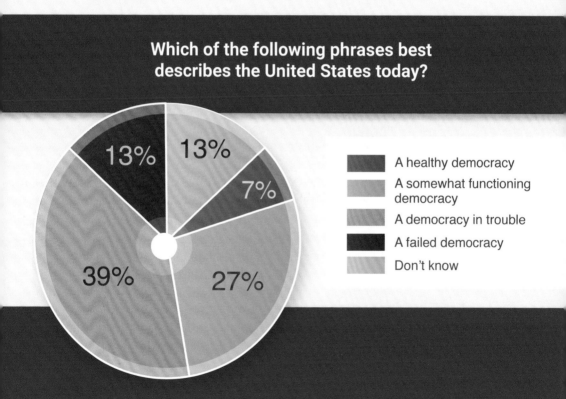

- 13% A healthy democracy
- A somewhat functioning democracy
- A democracy in trouble
- A failed democracy
- Don't know

13% 13% 7% 39% 27%

Source: "Harvard Youth Poll," Harvard Kennedy School Institute of Politics, December 1, 2021. https://iop.harvard.edu.

An Attack on the Government

On the afternoon of January 6, 2021, a man pointed at the US Capitol building and shouted into a loudspeaker, "We will take that building!"[1] Soon a mob broke past a line of police officers. Some members of the mob wore body armor. Some carried baseball bats, pepper spray, or Tasers. People jumped fences. They punched in windows and kicked in doors. The mob forced its way into the building. As staff barricaded doors with conference tables and sofas, members of the mob cheered and took photos and videos of themselves sitting in lawmakers' chairs.

Who were the people in this mob? They were Americans who came to Washington, DC, to support President Donald Trump. Lawmakers in the Capitol building were about to certify the results of the

> ★ "This election was a fraud."[2]
>
> —Donald Trump, former US president

presidential election that took place on November 3, 2020. President Joe Biden won that election. For months beforehand, Trump had claimed that Democrats would rig the election. Afterward, he falsely claimed, "This election was a fraud."[2] The phrase and hashtag "stop the steal" became a rallying cry for his supporters. They believed wholeheartedly that a crime had been committed. And some were willing to do whatever it took to get justice. Tragically, one police officer and several of the people who stormed the

Rioters storm the U.S. Capitol in an attempt to disrupt the certification by Congress of Joe Biden's victory in the 2020 presidential election.

Capitol Building lost their lives in the fighting. Over one hundred police officers were injured.

Democracy Wins

The election had not been stolen. Numerous government officials, judges, and other experts—many of them Republicans—agreed that votes had been cast and counted fairly. "The November 3rd election was the most secure in American history,"[3] said a joint statement from the Cybersecurity and Infrastructure Security Agency (CISA), the Election Infrastructure Government Coordinating Council, and the Election Infrastructure Sector Coordinating Council. The director of CISA at the time, Chris Krebs, said, "There was no indication or evidence . . . of hacking or compromise of election systems on, before, or after November 3."[4] (Krebs lost his job for telling the truth about the election.)

Trump's claims of fraud and the "stop the steal" memes spreading on social media were examples of disinformation. Disinformation includes lies and false or biased claims that are intended to deceive people. In this case that deception led to a direct assault on American democracy. Voting is at the heart of any democracy. Elections invite ordinary people to choose their city, state, and country's leadership and laws. The people trying to stop the lawmakers from certifying an election were disrupting an important step in the democratic process—because they believed disinformation.

In this case the rioters did not succeed, and disinformation did not defeat democracy. Just one day later, on January 7, the election result was certified. Mike Pence, vice president at the time, said, "To those who wreaked havoc in our Capitol today, you did not win. Violence never wins. Freedom wins, and this is still the people's house."[5]

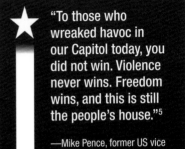

"To those who wreaked havoc in our Capitol today, you did not win. Violence never wins. Freedom wins, and this is still the people's house."[5]

—Mike Pence, former US vice president

The Threat Remains

Democracy may have prevailed this time. But disinformation remains a serious and growing threat to democratic governments around the world. Its partner in crime, misinformation, is also a big problem. Misinformation includes lies or false claims that are spread in error or without the realization that the information is deceptive.

Disinformation and misinformation are nothing new. In 1710 author Jonathan Swift wrote, "Falsehood flies, and the Truth comes limping after it."[6] But the ways people spread bad information today are quite new. Anyone can create a social media account (or many accounts) and spread messages that have the potential to reach the entire online world. False, misleading, and ignorant messages mix with accurate, honest, and well-researched messages in a sea of online noise. Meanwhile, new messages continually rain down from all directions. People scroll or tap through content at breakneck speed, rarely taking the time to think deeply about truth or deception.

At the same time, many people are losing their faith in experts and institutions. In the past, even Americans who disagreed on politics tended to agree that people such as scientists, doctors, judges, journalists, and many other types of experts were generally trustworthy. Information that came from venerated institutions, such as universities, research labs, and newspapers, was also generally trusted. This is no longer the case. Some even feel that we now live in a post-truth world, where facts no longer matter. In this world, people cannot share a common reality.

Informed decision-making about a common reality is at the foundation of a healthy democracy. Will bad information continue to erode this foundation? Or will attempts to counter "fake news" prevail?

CHAPTER ONE

Good Information Matters

A group of middle school students waved signs and chanted, "No more plastic bags! Do something drastic, cut the plastic!"[7] It was 2018, and these kids were part of an effort to ban plastic bags in the state of Vermont. Harper Wilson, a fifth grader at Manchester Elementary Middle School, had organized her friends to make signs and come together to protest. They were one small part of an effort to ban plastic bags and other types of single-use plastic in cities and states across the United States.

As part of this effort, activists of all ages and backgrounds shared information. They educated themselves about how plastic impacts the environment, especially the ocean. Much of this information came from scientists and experts who had conducted scientific research. Activists also came up with alternatives to plastic, such as reusable bags and paper or cardboard food containers. They researched the results of plastic bans in other cities and communities. Finally, they distributed information about plastic pollution and plastic alternatives using the media.

Meanwhile, companies that make or distribute plastic bags also made their voices heard. They had concerns about customer convenience and the cost of switching to paper products. Voters received all of these messages and considered which side's argument made the most sense to them.

In Vermont in 2019, people turned out to vote for plastic bans in several cities. Then the state government passed a law banning

This grey seal pup is chewing on a discarded plastic bag. Activists are trying to educate the public about the impact that single-use plastic bags have on the environment, and particularly the ocean.

not only single-use plastic bags but plastic stirrers and Styrofoam food and drink containers as well.

Democracy vs. Dictatorship

The story of Vermont's plastic ban illustrates how a democracy is supposed to work. Ordinary people saw a problem, raised awareness, and then voted to change the rules in their community. The definition of a democracy is a government in which people have the power to choose their own laws and leaders. A free flow of information is key to the democratic process.

To make free, democratic choices, people must inform themselves about the laws and leaders in question. They must thoroughly understand the issues and the candidates. The best and deepest understanding comes from consuming trustworthy information from a variety of different sources, as well as opinions from more than one side of an issue. Once voters have done their research, they can act in their own interest and in the interest of their family and community. They can make sure that they vote for the option that best aligns with their values, beliefs, and desires. They can also hold the government accountable and demand equal treatment and equal justice, says Laura Neuman, a lawyer at the Carter Center. She says that in a democracy, "information belongs to the people."[8]

To understand why access to quality information is so important in a democracy, it helps to look at a country where information does not flow freely. The country of North Korea is a dictatorship, meaning that one person has absolute power. There is no democracy there. One way that Kim Jong-un, the current supreme leader of the country, and his regime have stayed in power for so long is by carefully controlling the media that North Korean people are allowed to consume. From childhood, they are fed a version of reality that paints their supreme leader as an almost godlike being and casts foreign nations as untrustworthy and out to get them. Most North Koreans are desperately poor, yet this suffering is presented as noble, brave, and necessary for the good of the country. TVs and radios are pre-tuned to government-run stations. Anyone tuning in to a foreign broadcast may be punished. The only electronic devices allowed are ones that contain software that spies on the content the user accesses. The government can then find and punish people who are consuming or sharing any foreign media. The organization Reporters Without Borders ranks the countries of the world by their amount of press freedom each year. North Korea consistently sits at or near the very bottom of this list.

Authoritarian Governments

North Korea is a very extreme example. But many countries around the world have authoritarian governments that try to control people's beliefs and limit free speech. China and Russia are two examples. In these governments, one person or one small group has all the power. Members of both governments exert a lot of control over the media and paint a version of reality that makes themselves look strong and good. These governments also censor any unflattering news. Russia acts as a democracy and holds elections, but the elections are not free and fair.

Five Types of Bad Information

First Draft is a nonprofit organization that aims to protect people from bad information. It defines many different types of bad information. Here are five types to look out for.

False Context

This content includes mismatched text, images, or other media. For example, a story about a hurricane contains an old image from a different hurricane in a different location.

Misleading Information

This content contains facts that have been manipulated. For example, the context of a person's quote gets left out. Or statistics may be presented on a graph that makes a problem look much larger or smaller than it really is. This is especially common in advertising and political propaganda.

Imposter Content

This content uses logos or branding from respected news organizations or journalists in order to make false or misleading stories seem legitimate.

Manipulated Content

Real content, typically images or videos, are edited to change the meaning. In one example, an image of a school shooting survivor tearing a gun target in half was changed so that it appeared as if she was tearing the Constitution in half.

Fabricated Content

This is fake news. It is 100 percent false yet presented as real information.

Voters who live in a place without free media and free access to information can never really have the power to make choices for themselves because they are not allowed to hear outside perspectives about what is going on in their country or around the world. Even if they do manage to inform themselves, they usually are not allowed to organize any sort of protest or movement for change. The more disinformation citizens believe, the less free their choices become. They tend to make the choices that the people in power want them to make, rather than the choices that are best for themselves, their families, and their communities.

This is why disinformation is such an important challenge for democracy. It erodes people's ability to make informed choices and limits their power. If this goes too far, the government is no longer a democracy at all. In a democracy, "the sharing of quality information is important for people to make up their minds,"[9] says Claire Wardle. She is a researcher at First Draft, an institution working to combat what it calls "polluted information."[10]

Types of Information

In order to share quality information, people need to know how to recognize it. Information comes in many forms. It may be a tweet, article, image, video, or virtual reality experience. No matter the form, its purpose is always to update people's knowledge or understanding. Fictional stories, fantasies, and jokes—even when they are thought-provoking—are entertainment, not information. *Good information* refers to content that accurately reflects reality. Good information comes from direct experience, primary sources, or thorough research, such as scientific experiments or surveys. The author, editor, or distributor of the information has fact-checked its claims. The creator either attempts to be objective or makes it clear that the work contains opinions. The creator also clearly identifies any claims that require more evidence and may not turn out to be true.

Bad information is any information that does not accurately reflect reality but that people perceive as true. It includes both disinformation and misinformation. The difference between the two lies in the intentions of the person who created or distributed the information. Disinformation is created or shared with the intent to deceive people. If the information deceives people even though it was not meant to, it is called misinformation. For example, a newspaper called the *Onion* prints fake stories that are meant to be funny. Most people realize the information is fictional. As soon as someone misinterprets an *Onion* article as true, though, it becomes an example of misinformation.

The most dangerous and pervasive type of misinformation happens when a person believes something false or misleading, then spreads it among his or her social circle. That person thinks he or she is spreading something true and helpful, but in fact it is incorrect and harmful. This happened during the coronavirus pandemic. Some people believed and spread misinformation about drugs or treatments that were supposed to help prevent or cure COVID-19. They thought they were helping friends and family. In fact, most of the drugs and treatments did not help at all and even harmed some of the people who tried them.

Fake News and Propaganda

The people inventing and spreading disinformation are not so innocent. Some do this to make money. Fake stories drive clicks online, and this brings in income from online advertising. Governments, militaries, and corporations may put together campaigns of disinformation to try to control the public. One famous example is the Russian interference in US elections in 2016 and again in 2020. In both cases, Russia used disinformation to try to boost former president Donald Trump's image,

People receive and share information on their personal electronic devices but need to be able to recognize the quality of what they read and share.

A Fake News Empire

An organization called Natural News runs a fake news empire. A former employee, Robert Willis, came forward publicly in 2021 to blow the whistle on this company and its harmful practices. "I feel like I had to come forward unmasked to inform the public on how this news traveled, the mechanisms behind it, and the role I played," Willis says in a statement on his website. Willis worked for the company from 2015 to 2017.

The organization mostly promotes false or misleading health information. But it churned out pro-Trump and anti-Clinton content during the 2016 election. Willis helped the organization set up dozens of websites and Facebook accounts that seemed independent. In reality, he ran them all, and they all boosted the same problematic content. One reason Willis came forward is that the network has spread bad information about COVID-19. He believes this has led to people's deaths. His own father has refused to wear a mask or get vaccinated. "The new war is to wake up those who have been manipulated, while actively taking out fake news campaigns," he says.

Robert Willis, "Statement: 10/18/21," Robert Willis Hacking, October 18, 2021. https://robertwillis hacking.com.

Quoted in Ax Sharma. "'Hacker X'—the American Who Built a Pro-Trump Fake News Empire—Unmasks Himself," Ars Technica, October 14, 2021. https://arstechnica.com.

smear his opponents, and spread division and mistrust among Americans. It is unclear how much this interference impacted the outcome of either election. But the fact that it happened at all is disturbing.

The term *fake news* started becoming popular in 2016. At first it described a particularly astonishing type of disinformation: completely invented stories about things that never happened, including quotes that were never actually spoken. These are fictional stories distributed as factual ones. One example is a story from 2016 claiming that Pope Francis had endorsed Trump for president. This never happened. The website WTOE 5 News invented the story and even made up a false quote from the pope, according to the fact-checking website Snopes. Since then, fake news has taken on a life of its own. "The term fake news has become almost meaningless," says Wardle. "Certain politicians are saying that anything they don't like is fake news."[11] At that point,

she says, the term is merely an insult. The correct definition of *fake news* is content that is completely false.

A fake story about the pope may influence how some people vote, but in general changing minds is extremely difficult. One of the most dangerous types of disinformation in a democracy tries to get people not to vote at all. This can happen if bad actors manage to spread lies among supporters of a certain party about where, when, or how to vote. If enough people do not show up, that can swing an election. This tactic is called voter suppression, and it can directly disrupt democracy.

Douglass Mackey was arrested in 2021 for running a voter suppression scheme. In 2016, he had targeted people who supported Hillary Clinton with messages claiming that people could vote for Clinton via text or a social media hashtag. This was a hoax. The US Department of Justice has estimated that this scheme cost Clinton at least forty-nine hundred votes. When announcing the arrest, US Attorney Seth DuCharme said, "There is no place in public discourse for lies and misinformation to defraud citizens of their right to vote."[12]

Most disinformation is not entirely fake. Propaganda is a very common example. Propaganda is any false, misleading, or biased information created to support a certain point of view. For example, in 2020 the Trump campaign released a TV ad showing an elderly woman who calls 911 as someone breaks into her home, but no one is available to help her. The ad says,

"You won't be safe in Joe Biden's America."[13] Biden did say he would support reforming police departments. However, he is against defunding the police. Also, those people who do hope to defund police plan to make sure that families can still get help from 911 during emergencies. This ad is propaganda because it twists the truth and triggers people's fears. Propaganda is nothing new. Politicians all over the world and all throughout human history have used lies and misleading claims to make their opponents look bad and themselves look better.

Fighting the Lies

In a healthy democracy, politicians are not the only source of information. The media report on events large and small, national and local. They often fact-check statements made by politicians and other people in positions of influence. Journalists also investigate powerful people and companies to reveal corruption. Scientific institutions and think tanks conduct research, surveys, and analyses. People have many trusted resources to turn to in order to educate themselves. New laws and best practices can help limit the amount of bad information making it out into the world.

A healthy democracy also supports an education system that teaches people how to think critically about information, a skill called media literacy. People with strong media literacy skills seek out, consume, and create good information while avoiding and condemning bad information. They think deeply and critically about claims and demand expertise or evidence. They also know how to make their own voices heard. In a true democracy, the voices of all people matter. And that means providing all people with access to good information.

CHAPTER TWO

Tap, Like, Share

A cute puppy slides across a slippery floor. A scientist demonstrates how a disease spreads. A political candidate explains how she will cut taxes. A friend shows off a fruit salad that looks like a rainbow. Each video clip is just a few seconds to a minute long. Funny, shocking, serious, and mundane posts mingle together.

As individuals scroll through TikTok, Twitter, and other social media platforms, are they thinking deeply about each post? Are they wondering about the content creator's sources or expertise, or whether the creator might be an automated bot? Are they questioning whether the information is accurate? Almost definitely not. Most people scroll without thinking critically about whether a post is truthful, shaky, dubious, or fake. There is no time to do that. New messages are constantly flooding in. Users on their phones spend an average of just 1.7 seconds looking at a piece of content on Facebook before moving on, according to the company's data from 2016. People tap "like" or "share" or "comment" whenever something grabs their attention or provokes strong emotions. It is often a gut reaction.

This is not a huge problem if people are using social media solely for entertainment. Cute puppy videos are great fun. No one has to think deeply about that. But plenty of people use social media as a way to spread and consume important information as well. According to a 2019 survey by the Pew Research Center, over half of the adults in the United States get news from social media often or sometimes. While many of these news posts contain good information, others contain lies and propaganda. Misinformation and disinformation run rampant on most social media sites.

A Vessel for Democracy

The internet, social media, and mobile technology have each fundamentally changed the way people interact with information. The internet has made almost all of the information humankind has ever created available to anybody with access. Much of this information is free and searchable in an instant. Social media has made it possible for anybody with an account to share information with the rest of the online world. Citizens have become broadcasters. "The new media, including social media, allows anybody to say anything to everyone in the whole world for free,"[14] says Russell Muirhead, coauthor of *A Lot of People Are Saying: The New Conspiracism and the Assault on Democracy*. Finally, mobile technology has made it possible to carry all the world's information and the means to capture and broadcast new information around in a pocket. Anyone with the right technology can access or share information from anywhere, at any time.

A TikTok subscriber accesses the app on her smart phone. Research indicates that over half of American adults often get their news from social media.

From this description, new technology seems like the perfect vessel for democracy. The freedom of information and the sharing of ideas is what democracy is all about. In fact, new technology has supported democracy in many important ways. "Social media could serve as a source of live, raw information. It could summon people to the streets and coordinate their movements in real time,"[15] writes journalist Philip Montgomery. It could also push back against the stories the government or the media tried to tell about current events.

This happened during the Black Lives Matter movement in the summer of 2020. The media and the government were not telling the stories of Black people's suffering at the hands of police. Many people took to social media to share their outrage and demand change. This became a democratic movement to confront and repair injustices in society.

Protesters take part in a march in New York City in 2016 supporting the Black Lives Matter movement. Social media helped Black Lives Matter become a democratic movement to confront and repair injustices.

A Vessel for Manipulation

However, technology is a tool, and like any tool, it can be used in good or bad ways. Social media and mobile technology can help democracy when used to spread truths, but they can just as easily harm democracy when used to spread lies. Powerful people around the world have figured out how to use this technology to manipulate others. In fact, it is now easier than ever before to spread disinformation.

Many experts argue that on the whole, the rise of social media and mobile technology has been bad for democracy. "These changes to the way we communicate have weakened democracies and strengthened authoritarian regimes,"[16] writes Samuel Woolley in his book, *The Reality Game*. He says that governments are not the only ones misusing social media. Corporations, special interest groups, intelligence agencies, and even wealthy individuals use social media "in attempts to manipulate not only what we read, see, hear, and watch online but also how we feel and what we believe,"[17] he says.

> "These changes to the way we communicate have weakened democracies and strengthened authoritarian regimes."[16]
>
> —Samuel Woolley, author of *The Reality Game*

Social media platforms are perfect for spreading disinformation. One reason is that content of all kinds jumbles together in a person's feed. A message from an experienced medical doctor about the need to vaccinate against COVID-19 may appear next to a personal story claiming that a crystal warded off sickness. One message is the result of countless hours of research and investigation. The other is mere superstition. But both posts are presented in the same way and have the same opportunity for likes and shares.

The information presented on TV or radio news or in newspapers is organized and curated. At media businesses that seek to inform the public, editors decide which stories are worthy of the most attention, and fact-checkers help ensure truthfulness. An organization's reputation may be at stake if it fails to report the news honestly and accurately. Social media is very different. The people who run Facebook, Twitter, or TikTok do not directly select or create content—their users create and share everything. A computer program called an algorithm sorts out which content should appear front and center on each user's feed.

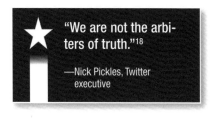

Social media companies do moderate their platforms, especially to remove hate speech and other harmful or illegal content. But they have been reluctant to get involved in weeding out all forms of bad information. "We are not the arbiters of truth,"[18] Nick Pickles, a Twitter executive, said in 2018. Facebook chief executive officer Mark Zuckerberg repeated those words in 2020, saying that he believed his company "shouldn't be the arbiter of truth of everything that people say online."[19]

A Popularity Contest

The goal of a social media company is not to inform the public. It is to keep users online and interacting as long as possible. That is because these companies make their money by gathering user information and targeting users with ads. As a result, what rises to the top on a social media site is not what is true or important but what is popular. It is the content that the most people have tapped, liked, or shared. The algorithms also personalize people's feeds. Each user sees the popular content that is most similar to what he or she liked or shared in the past.

People do share useful and informative stories. But the stories that become the most popular or even go viral, reaching millions, almost always spark strong emotions. Marketing expert and author Jonah Berger has found that "the more an experience provokes activating emotions, the more likely people are to share it."[20] Activating emotions, ones that make the heart race and get us ready to act, include wonder, surprise, anger, fear, and disgust.

Black Lives Matter

Darnella Frazier was just seventeen years old in 2020 when she shot a cell phone video of a police officer holding a knee against George Floyd's neck until he died. In the past, when cell phones and social media did not exist, it would have been difficult to prove that the police had acted wrongly. It would have been even more difficult to distribute evidence widely without the support of major media institutions. Thanks to new technology, the video went viral on social media, kicking off Black Lives Matter protests all over the United States. These protests led to new efforts to help prevent police brutality and racism in cities and states all across the nation. Frazier won a Pulitzer Prize for her bravery in recording and reporting Floyd's killing. Social media and mobile technology have given Frazier and others like her a voice.

Content that triggers sadness or other calmer emotions is less likely to spread. Facebook's algorithm amplifies this human tendency, according to an investigation by several news organizations. Emoji reactions (love, anger, sadness, surprise, and so on) to Facebook posts are treated as five times more valuable than mere "likes."

The creators of fake news and disinformation know exactly how to take advantage of people's emotions. Whenever content spreads widely, no matter how true it is, the content creators and the social media platform both benefit. "[Facebook] has profited off spreading misinformation and disinformation and sowing hate,"[21] said Senator Richard Blumenthal of Connecticut during a meeting about consumer protection.

> "[Facebook] has profited off spreading misinformation and disinformation and sowing hate."[21]
>
> —Richard Blumenthal, senator from Connecticut

Falsehood Flies

Even accidental misinformation, such as a rumor or mistake, spreads widely when it seems like important, breaking news. This happened after the bombings at the Boston Marathon in 2013. Rumors spread on Twitter about other explosions that never happened.

People injured in an explosion lie in the street near the finish line of the 2013 Boston Marathon. Rumors that ultimately proved to be false quickly spread on Twitter about other explosions.

This incident prompted Sinan Aral and a team of researchers at the MIT Sloan School of Management to look into how information spreads on Twitter. They found something astonishing. "We found that falsehood diffuses significantly farther, faster, deeper, and more broadly than the truth, in all categories of information,"[22] says Aral. Tweets containing false information were 70 percent more likely to be retweeted.

Strong emotions such as surprise and disgust only partly explained this. "False news is more novel, and people are more likely to share novel information,"[23] says Aral. In addition, seeing that thousands of people have liked or shared something makes that information seem more valid and accepted, even if it is actually completely false. Computer algorithms do not help the situation, either. They have no understanding of what any content means. "They treat something that's blatantly false the same way they would treat something that's accurate or uplifting,"[24] says Renée DiResta, a researcher at the Stanford Internet Observatory.

Bot Armies

It is not just humans and social media algorithms spreading disinformation on social media. Popularity can be manufactured in some very sneaky ways. Bots are accounts that send out automated or scheduled messages. Some are open about being bots and provide useful information such as weather updates. Other bots have names and profile pictures, but they are not real individuals. A person or group created them and controls them in order to spread a certain message. These imposter bots are another important reason that social media is a breeding ground for disinformation.

Astroturfing is the term for a disinformation campaign that disguises itself as a grassroots movement among real people. (That is because AstroTurf is fake grass). In fact, it is a movement composed of armies of bots that boost the reach of messages. They do this by posting and resharing disinformation or repeating hashtags. Eventually, real people and even the media may catch on and spread the message as well, often never realizing it originated with bots. Bots can also inflate follower counts, making it seem as if politicians or other leaders have more support than they really do. Finally, bots can be used to attack people. They may harass real people who are trying to spread good information, drowning out their voices or even bullying them into silence.

When Russia interfered in the US elections in 2016 and 2020, it often used bots and astroturfing. The Internet Research Agency in the Russian city of St. Petersburg was behind most of these attacks, according to US intelligence. In 2018 Twitter found 3,841 bot accounts associated with this group. The bots typically impersonated American voters, candidates, and political groups. They often used names and logos very similar to existing groups. In September 2019 an Instagram account called iowa.patriot posted an image promoting Trump for president. It seemed like an innocent political statement from an American voter. But the account was later traced to the Internet Research Agency. Other posts from Russian bots were not so innocent. Many were hateful or shocking, playing on people's emotions.

Personal Data

The final reason why disinformation campaigns work so well on social media is the fact that these platforms capture so much information about their users. Social media advertisers pay to target people by age, gender, location, marital status, occupation, and much more. The people running a disinformation campaign can pose as advertisers and target specific people with the lies most likely to fool them. Or they can just steal people's data.

In a famous scandal, the company Cambridge Analytica put up a personality quiz on Facebook. In 2015, 270,000 people took the quiz and got paid a few dollars. What they did not know is that Cambridge Analytica had gotten more than just their quiz answers. It had grabbed their personal data and all their friends' data, too. The company wound up with data on over 50 million Facebook users. The Trump campaign used this data to target people with political advertising.

Political advertising is a normal part of an election cycle. Propaganda abounds on both sides. What was not normal here was the fact that many of the people receiving ads via Cambridge Analytica's data set had never given consent for their personal information to be used. It is one thing to sit through political ads on the radio or TV. It is another to have those messages sneak into your personal social media in a form that has been designed to appeal to you specifically. "Computers are getting to a stage where in some senses, they might know us better than we know ourselves,"[25] says Katherine Mansted, a cybersecurity expert at the Australian National University National Security College. People who receive these types of targeted, personalized messages may not realize that their beliefs and choices are being manipulated.

In the future, new forms of technology, including deepfakes and virtual reality, could make bad information even worse. Deepfakes are video or audio files that have been fabricated or modified to contain events that never happened or quotes that were

Fighting Deepfakes

"We're entering an era in which our enemies can make it look like anyone is saying anything at any point in time, even if they would never say those things." This quote comes from a deepfake video circulated in 2018. Former president Barack Obama seems to say the words, but in fact they came from the mouth of actor Jordan Peele. A production company used face-swapping tools to combine the video of Peele with a video of Obama talking. This deepfake video was created openly to educate the public. But other faked videos are deceptive. People can no longer simply accept video footage as real without making sure it comes from a reliable source. This allows powerful people to create new realities or cast doubt on truthful video content. Even if humans cannot easily tell a real video from a fake one, researchers have built software that can do this. The organization Trusted News Initiative is using this software to authenticate videos.

Quoted in Craig Silverman. "How to Spot a Deepfake like the Barack Obama–Jordan Peele Video," BuzzFeed, April 17, 2018. www.buzzfeed.com.

never uttered. Although this technology can be used to create disinformation, it has an even scarier side. Powerful people who want to hide bad behavior can now claim that real video or audio has been doctored and is not actually real.

Virtual and augmented reality turn media into a whole-body experience. This type of experience tends to be more impactful and memorable than text, images, or video, so it could be even more harmful. It may also be possible to create fake virtual people who are puppets for disinformation campaigns but seem entirely real. Society must prepare for this future with regulation and also education. As Woolley writes, "We need scientists who understand social problems and policymakers who understand technology."[26]

CHAPTER THREE

A Post-Truth World

It is tempting to blame new technology for causing the current crisis of disinformation. But the situation is not that simple. Disinformation started becoming a threat long before social media and mobile devices existed. Over the past decades, America's political parties have grown apart into two extremely contrasting groups, a state called political polarization. In a polarized society, the two opposing groups have trouble finding any common ground for productive debate or constructive governing. Some members of the groups feel that the other side is dangerous or evil. Disinformation feeds this bubbling hatred and grows out of it as well.

US politics has two main groups: Democrats, also called liberals or the left, and Republicans, also called conservatives or the right. Today's political parties have become a form of personal identity. Many people find it easier to trust, respect, and love those who identify with the same party, and they feel distrust, fear, or hate for those of the opposite party. In 1960 just 4 percent of Republicans and 4 percent of Democrats would have been unhappy if their child married someone of the opposite party. Those percentages had jumped to 45 percent of Democrats and 35 percent of Republicans as of 2017. In recent years this polarization has extended into almost every aspect of life—including public health during the coronavirus pandemic. Some experts argue that our society has entered into something truly troubling—a post-truth world.

In a post-truth world, truth itself is broken. People do not accept that a common reality or facts about that reality exist. "My fear is that we're losing a belief that there are facts,"[27] says Claire Wardle. When facts cannot be trusted, emotions take precedence over reasoned thinking, and opinions or beliefs are all that matter. "When the information stream is polluted with false stories, people can become cynical and stop believing that there's any such thing as truth at all,"[28] says Lee C. McIntyre, author of the book *Post-Truth*. If we are indeed living in a post-truth world, then how did we get here?

How Polarization Happened

The first question to answer is how Democrats and Republicans grew to distrust each other so much that they can no longer agree on basic facts about the world. According to the authors of the book *Network Propaganda*, the current polarization in American politics is partly due to social upheaval. This began with the civil rights movement in the 1960s and continued with movements for women's rights, sexual freedom and abortion rights, gay rights, and more. The left tended to attract people who supported these movements, while the right tended to attract those who felt their values and identities were at risk, including many evangelical Christians. Growing economic inequality fed the division as well.

The media has played a big role in increasing polarization. Even before the internet or social media existed, media outlets discovered that hate and outrage sell. The Federal Communications Commission once had a rule called the fairness doctrine. Under this doctrine, TV and radio broadcasters had to provide their audiences with balanced coverage of controversial issues. In 1987 the doctrine was repealed because people argued that it limited free speech. Soon afterward, talk radio and TV shows that riled up listeners sprang up like mushrooms after a rainstorm. They became hugely popular.

Protesters gathered in large numbers for the March on Washington in August 1963. In the decades since the civil rights movement began, mass media outlets have discovered that hate and outrage can be used to increase the popularity of talk radio and TV shows.

Matt Taibbi, author of the book *Hate Inc.*, argues that outlets such as Fox News and MSNBC brought Americans a new kind of news and a new kind of politics. Their news programs were more like a boxing match than a debate. By the 2016 election, he writes, compromise was no longer an option. "Your team either won or lost, and you felt devastated or vindicated accordingly. We were training rooters instead of readers,"[29] he writes. People learned not to think deeply about stories but to cheer on their own side and boo the other side.

Online this division has only gotten worse. People tend to form communities called echo chambers. "If people interact constructively, I would give you my opinion, and you would give me yours, then we would meet in the middle,"[30] says Fabian Baumann, a physicist at Humboldt University of Berlin in Germany who has mapped online echo chambers. But in an echo chamber, everyone repeats the same kinds of ideas. As everyone agrees with these ideas, the entire group feels even more attached to that way of thinking. They all move further from the middle. The algorithms that suggest content also tend to push people toward ever more extreme views, because extreme emotion keeps people engaged and online longer.

Casting Doubt

Post-truth politics, polarization, and echo chambers make it much easier to spread bad information. However, this is only part of the danger. In a post-truth world, people also reject good information. Powerful people are intentionally casting doubt on truths or institutions that are sources of truth. As a result, people may not agree on whether an event or statement did or did not happen.

Here is an example: how big was the crowd at President Trump's inauguration in 2017? There should be no gray area here. A specific number of people attended the event. It should not be hard to estimate how many from images or other available data. Yet some people do not agree on an answer to that question. Here is why: soon after the event, Trump's administration claimed that the event had attracted the largest crowd ever. Photographs and other evidence showed that this was a false claim. But Trump's team did not back down. Kellyanne Conway, Trump's senior counselor, said the administration's claim was based on "alternative facts,"[31] the first use of a term that is central to a post-truth way of thinking.

To Mask or Not to Mask?

Political polarization can have devastating results. During the coronavirus pandemic, the science was pretty clear that wearing a mask could protect individuals and those around them. This should have been a public safety issue, not a political issue. "Wearing a mask is not a political statement," wrote Christine Peters, a microbiologist. But despite the best efforts of Peters and other health experts, many conservatives denounced masks as an unnecessary affront to personal freedom. One group even encouraged people to burn masks in protest. In a Pew Research Center poll from June 2020, 76 percent of Democrats and just 53 percent of Republicans reported wearing a mask in public all or most of the time. Vaccination rates have also been higher among Democrats than among Republicans. The parties refused to share a common reality with common facts even about something as terrible as a pandemic. The realities they chose strongly opposed each other. This polarization resulted in hospitalizations and deaths that did not have to happen.

Christine Peters, "'Wearing a Mask Is Not a Political Statement,'" *New Statesman*, September 8, 2021. www.newstatesman.com.

Supporters crowd the National Mall in Washington, DC, for the inauguration of Donald Trump in January 2017. Members of Trump's administration falsely claimed that his inauguration attracted the largest crowd ever to attend such an event.

Some say that Trump transformed the Republican Party into something that is very typical of authoritarian governments—a cult of personality. For example, Charlie Dent, a former Republican representative, says, "The fringe elements of the party have too large a voice . . . it's a cult of personality."[32] A cult of personality happens when a person in power gets only praise and adoration from followers. The followers believe this powerful person can do no wrong and will twist the truth to support that person. They will also deny or distrust information coming from any outside sources.

A Lack of Trust

Many Americans no longer know whom to trust. The institutions and organizations that used to provide objective knowledge—universities, government agencies, large newspapers, and more—have lost much of their authority. Online their voices must compete with everyone else's. "Truth is no longer dictated by authorities, but is networked by peers. For every fact there is a counterfact and all these counterfacts and facts look identical online, which is confusing to most people,"[33] says Kevin Kelly, cofounder of *Wired* magazine.

In addition, Americans have been told again and again not to trust these authorities. Over the course of Trump's presidency, he attacked the media many times. This was not a new tactic. Fox News began accusing the media of a liberal bias in the early 2000s. This all culminated in 2019, when Trump called the entire free press "the enemy of the people."[34] Trump was actively discrediting the entire institution of journalism.

A 2020 Gallup poll found that just 9 percent of Americans had a great deal of trust in the mass media, while 31 percent had a fair amount of trust. When they divided respondents by political party, though, they found polarization. Since Trump was elected president, trust in the media has dropped among Republicans and stayed fairly steady among Democrats. Trust in the government has also been dropping over time. In 1958 around 75 percent of Americans trusted that the federal government would do the right thing all the time or most of the time. That proportion has been at 30 percent or less since 2007, according to the Pew Research Center.

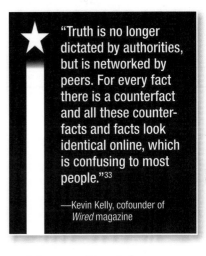

"Truth is no longer dictated by authorities, but is networked by peers. For every fact there is a counterfact and all these counterfacts and facts look identical online, which is confusing to most people."[33]

—Kevin Kelly, cofounder of *Wired* magazine

Science is one institution that has managed to mostly retain the public's trust. From 2016 through 2019, the portion of Americans who reported that they have a great deal or a fair amount of trust in scientists to do the right thing rose from 76 percent to 86 percent, according to the Pew Research Center. On certain issues, though, attacks on the facts of science are a huge problem. Climate change is one of those issues. It is a fact that climate change is happening, and humans helped cause it. However, conservatives tend to deny that the problem exists or that

Mass Media: Trust and Distrust

Years of being told not to trust the mass media—newspapers, television, and radio—may have had an effect on American attitudes toward the media. A 2020 Gallup poll found that trust in the media to provide full, fair, and accurate news reporting has fallen over time. When broken down by political party, however, trust in media has moved in radically different directions. The poll reveals a steep decline in trust among Republicans, a smaller decline among Independents, but a significant rise in trust among Democrats.

American's Trust in Mass Media, by Political Party

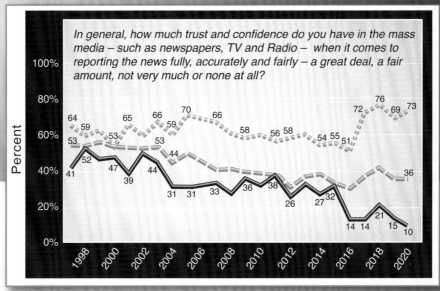

Source: Megan Brenan, "Americans Remain Distrustful of Mass Media," Gallup, September 30, 2020. https://news.gallup.com.

humans caused it. Sometimes they accuse scientists of lying. Liberals distrust some types of science, too. For example, some feel that it is unsafe to consume genetically modified foods, even though science has shown they are perfectly safe to eat.

When powerful leaders are telling the public that it is okay to disbelieve scientific facts, that is a huge problem. Neil deGrasse Tyson, an astrophysicist and popular science communicator, says, "It's not something to say 'I choose not to believe $E = mc^2$.' You don't have that option." Scientific facts are real information about the world that all humans share. They are not open to interpretation. Tyson says that when people deny science and urge others to do the same, "that is a recipe for the complete dismantling of our informed democracy."[35]

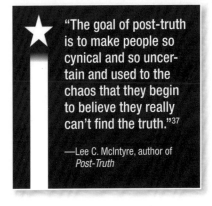

"The goal of post-truth is to make people so cynical and so uncertain and used to the chaos that they begin to believe they really can't find the truth."[37]

—Lee C. McIntyre, author of *Post-Truth*

Confusion and Disempowerment

Disinformation that casts doubt or denies truths is possibly even more damaging than outright lies and propaganda. Russell Muirhead and his coauthor Nancy L. Rosenblum call it conspiracism. "It takes a world that is shared, that is transparent, and makes one that is very disorienting, confusing, and disempowering,"[36] says Muirhead. Often, conspiracism confuses and disorients people until they do not know what to believe anymore. McIntyre says, "The goal of post-truth is to make people so cynical and so uncertain and used to the chaos that they begin to believe they really can't find the truth."[37] When this

The QAnon Conspiracy

When disinformation and post-truth thinking reign, conspiracy theories spread more easily. A conspiracy theory is an alternate explanation for an event or series of events. This explanation may seem crazy to outsiders. For example, one conspiracy theory claims that the earth is flat. Around the time Donald Trump took office, a new conspiracy began spreading online. It involved online posts from an anonymous person who used the name "Q" and claimed to work inside the US government.

Q's posts were always cryptic, but followers of Q came up with explanations. The basic idea of the QAnon conspiracy is that many powerful people in the world are part of a group that abuses children. Trump was supposedly elected to break up this group and bring justice to its leaders, which supposedly include many top Democrats, celebrities, and even some religious leaders. No reliable evidence has ever been found to support any part of this conspiracy theory. Yet a 2021 poll found that 15 percent of Americans—around 30 million people—believe in it. Some believe so strongly that they are willing to take action. QAnon leaders helped organize the insurrection at the US Capitol on January 6, 2021.

happens, people may feel that things are hopeless. They may stop participating in democracy.

Unfortunately, this tactic is working. Fadi Quran of the social advocacy group Avaaz says that minorities in particular have been attacked with a particularly cruel type of disinformation. "[It] will seek to make you feel frustrated, feel like your voice doesn't matter, feel like your society is broken, with the purpose of making you say, I'm not going to go vote. It doesn't matter who I vote for."[38] Such feelings of hopelessness and cynicism lead to real disempowerment when they impact voting behavior.

Confusion about facts makes it difficult for everyone to participate in democracy, because people cannot properly inform themselves. Disagreement and debate are normal parts of democracy. However, when people cannot establish common ground and share facts about the world, they cannot work together, compromise, or even disagree respectfully. Democracy requires trust, respect, clear understanding, and activism. Post-truth politics and polarization decrease all of these things and enhance fear, hatred, confusion, and apathy. This is very dangerous to democracy. "The lack of trust and the division and the polarization that can be driven by disinformation can be hugely damaging,"[39] says Katherine Mansted.

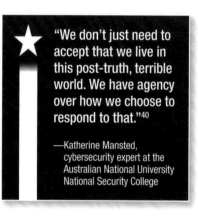

"We don't just need to accept that we live in this post-truth, terrible world. We have agency over how we choose to respond to that."[40]

—Katherine Mansted, cybersecurity expert at the Australian National University National Security College

It is important to find a way to return to a world where truth matters and everyone shares a common reality. "We don't just need to accept that we live in this post-truth, terrible world. We have agency over how we choose to respond to that,"[40] says Mansted. Thankfully, many smart and passionate people are working on this response. They are finding ways to combat disinformation.

CHAPTER FOUR

Stopping the Lies

One way to stop misinformation and disinformation is at the source. The fewer lies people tell and the less often those lies get repeated, the better information everyone will have. It would be great if politicians, governments, businesses, and other powerful people never lied, exaggerated, or used propaganda. But this is an unreasonable expectation. It is human nature to resort to these types of tactics when trying to persuade others. Plus, all people have the right to speak their minds and share their opinions. The reasonable expectation is that powerful people should be held accountable when they twist the truth.

The media is the institution responsible for keeping powerful people in check. When a free and open media is doing its job, powerful people have an incentive to be mostly honest. They know that if they act dishonestly and the truth comes out, their reputation could be ruined. Depending on how terrible their dishonesty was, they may even face fines or jail time. Traditional media—TV, radio, and newspapers—are not perfect gatekeepers of the truth. But the most reputable organizations have generally done a good job of getting the facts straight, looking at both sides of an issue, and striving for fair, thorough reporting.

In contrast, social media has been like the Wild West. There are almost no sheriffs watching over everything. In some ways this is a good thing because voices that had been left out of traditional media now have a way to reach audiences. However, it is a terrible thing when powerful people and powerful groups rampage like outlaws, spreading bad information—or distrust in good information—far and wide.

How can society stop the lies? First of all, good journalism still exists and can still hold people accountable for disinformation. Second, social media companies can take strides to reduce the amount of fake and misleading news on their platforms. Finally, organizations concerned with supporting democracy and confronting disinformation have ideas for how to take this progress even further.

Supporting Ethical Journalism

One way to confront disinformation is with good information. That information typically comes from journalists working for established newspapers, news websites, radio stations, podcasts, and TV stations. Investigative journalism is like detective work. Good journalists work methodically and carefully to uncover injustice and bring deception to light. The Code of Ethics of the Society of Professional Journalists reads, "Ethical journalism should be ac-

In the process of crafting interesting, informative, and accurate news stories, the best journalists work carefully and methodically as they gather information, double check sources, and obtain comments from those who are affected by the events at the center of their stories.

curate and fair. Journalists should be honest and courageous in gathering, reporting and interpreting information."[41]

Journalists do not work alone. A team of editors and fact-checkers help make sure that a story is as accurate as possible. This includes calling multiple sources separately to make sure everyone's version of reality agrees. Rebecca Aguilar, president of the Society of Professional Journalists, has worked as a TV news reporter. She says her bosses would always ask her multiple times, "Where did you get this? How do you know?"[42] They double-checked and triple-checked everything.

Americans want quality news. The same Gallup poll that found very low levels of trust in the media also found that 80 percent of Americans believe that the news media is critical or very important to democracy. So it seems that Americans do not feel like the media is doing its job. In many ways, that is a very fair criticism. Journalism as an industry is struggling. It is expensive to produce quality stories. Many small, local news outlets have closed as subscribers

"I am worried about the future of quality news and how accessible that news is."[43]

—Michael Luo, editor at the *New Yorker*

and advertisers have stopped supporting them. Meanwhile, online news sites are producing huge numbers of "click-bait" stories very quickly and very cheaply. This type of media is often inaccurate or misleading. "The sheer number of people who gather the information that has potential for [supporting] democracy has dwindled," says Michael Luo, an editor at the *New Yorker*. "I am worried about the future of quality news and how accessible that news is."[43] The news media has to start doing a better job of producing quality information and getting that information into the hands of the people who want it.

Taming the Wild West

The efforts of ethical journalists and the voices of citizens with real concerns are all too easily drowned out online, especially on social media. "It doesn't have to be the way that it is. It's that way because of design choices,"[44] says Katherine Mansted. Facebook, Twitter, and other similar platforms have taken some steps to alter their design and clean up the information on their sites. The goal is to reduce disinformation without limiting free speech.

Twitter's main strategy has been to hunt for and remove malicious bot accounts. However, Twitter will also remove content that contains hate speech or false information that could lead to risk of harm. After the insurrection at the US Capitol in January 2021, the company permanently suspended Trump's account because his tweets had helped incite the violence.

The News Media Is Not the Enemy

When Donald Trump called the news media "the enemy of the people" in 2018, more than 350 newspapers and other organizations responded. They published editorials defending the work they do. With heartfelt pride, they explained how seriously they take their job of keeping the public informed. Below are excerpts from three of those editorials.

"Citizens depend on honest, independent media for accurate information they need about their government, their elected leaders and their institutions."
— The *Tampa Bay Times*

"Like any true friend, we don't always tell you what you want to hear. . . . And like any true friend, we refuse to mislead you. Our reporters and editors strive for fairness."
— The *Savannah Morning News*

"If you haven't already, please subscribe to your local papers. Praise them when you think they've done a good job and criticize them when you think they could do better. We're all in this together."
— The *New York Times*

Tampa Bay (FL) Times, "Editorial: Journalists Are Friends of Democracy, Not the Enemy," August 16, 2018. www.tampabay.com.

Quoted in David Bauder, "US Newspapers to Trump: We're Not Enemies of the People," AP, August 16, 2018. https://apnews.com.

New York Times, "A Free Press Needs You," August 15, 2018. www.nytimes.com.

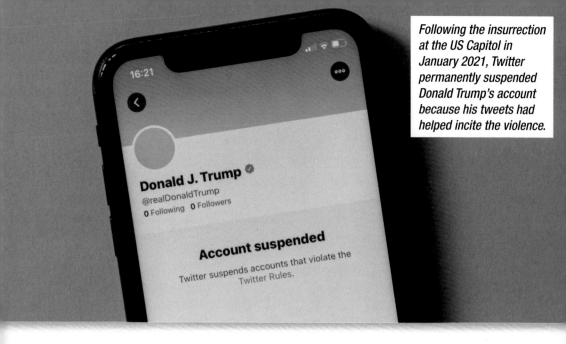

However, disinformation that does not directly lead to harm is allowed. Warning labels may be applied to some false or deceptive posts. Twitter ramped up these efforts in 2020 to try to prevent people from tampering with the US election. Labeled tweets were not recommended by the algorithm, and users faced a pop-up warning if they tried to share the information. In a statement, Twitter said, "We're working to ensure we are surfacing the highest quality and most relevant content and context first."[45]

Facebook has hired moderators and fact-checkers from outside companies. Users can also report content. If Facebook determines that a post is harmful, it gets removed. If it is merely false, moderators apply labels. In the months leading up to the 2020 US election, they put these labels on 180 million posts. However, the labels Facebook has placed on disinformation do not seem to have worked very well. A Facebook data scientist told BuzzFeed News in 2020 that these labels only decreased resharing by about 8 percent. That is not a lot.

More Work to Be Done

Many experts say social media companies—especially Facebook— have not done nearly enough to combat disinformation.

41

"Facebook's attempts to control the epidemic of misleading information on its platforms are nothing more than performative PR exercises,"[46] says Imran Ahmed, chief executive officer of the Center for Countering Digital Hate.

In 2021, after false information about COVID-19 and vaccines had spread on Facebook, many people were calling for change. "Facebook needs to move more quickly to remove harmful, violative posts. Posts that will be within their policy for removal often remain up for days. That's too long,"[47] said White House press secretary Jen Psaki. A 2020 report from New York University's Stern Center for Business and Human Rights recommended that Facebook double the number of moderators it employs and expand its fact-checking efforts, too.

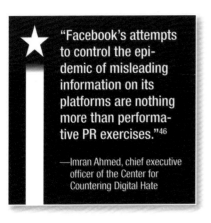

"Facebook's attempts to control the epidemic of misleading information on its platforms are nothing more than performative PR exercises."[46]

—Imran Ahmed, chief executive officer of the Center for Countering Digital Hate

Former researchers at Facebook have come forward to say that they conducted many studies in 2018 that showed that maximizing engagement meant increasing polarization on the platform. Facebook was not willing to let engagement drop, so the company did nothing in response to these studies. "When you're in the business of maximizing engagement, you're not interested in truth. You're not interested in harm, divisiveness, conspiracy. In fact, those are your friends,"[48] says Hany Farid of the University of California, Berkeley.

Another issue is that social media companies lack transparency. That means they do not share very much of their data with researchers or with the government. So it is very difficult for experts to study how disinformation gets created and spread on these platforms. TV and radio broadcasters are required to report the ads that political groups buy on their platforms to the Federal Communications Commission. Experts have argued that Facebook and other social media platforms should be required to do this also. "The democratic process is harmed when Americans don't know who is attempting to influence them via political ads,"[49] writes strategist Nancy Watzman for the Democracy Fund.

Social media companies also keep the inner workings of their algorithms secret. Experts have suggested that they should be required to make this information available to outside researchers. These researchers could then analyze how algorithms contribute to the spread of disinformation and how they might be improved. Safety standards, rules, and regulations for social media mostly do not exist, and many argue that these are needed. "I have to do more safety testing and go through more compliance procedures to create a toaster than to create Facebook,"[50] says Christopher Wylie, the whistle-blower who revealed the Cambridge Analytica scandal to the public.

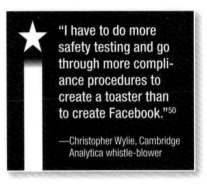

"I have to do more safety testing and go through more compliance procedures to create a toaster than to create Facebook."[50]

—Christopher Wylie, Cambridge Analytica whistle-blower

Full, Free, and Fair Speech

Regulation of social media can be a slippery slope. Many conservatives have claimed that social media is biased against them.

Former researchers at Facebook say that studies conducted in 2018 showed that increasing polarization would help maximize user engagement.

Whether or not this is the case, it is true that some governments around the world have censored social media in order to silence certain voices and control public opinion. In America free speech is guaranteed under the Constitution. However, no one is guaranteed free reach to a wide audience or free amplification by an algorithm. "Nobody has that right," says Renée DiResta, a researcher at the Stanford Internet Observatory. "That is not a part of the first amendment... You have never had the right to free mass dissemination."[51] In other words, no one has the right to use armies of bots and trolls to artificially boost their speech.

Heidi Tworek is an expert in public policy and history at the University of British Columbia in Canada. She says that people have a right to "full, free, and fair participation in politics and political debates."[52] The *full* part means that every voice should be included. *Free* means that people can say whatever they want, as long as it is not hateful or threatening violence. *Fair* is the tricky part, but it includes transparency about the source and truthfulness of information.

Even organizations that make it their mission to fight disinformation understand the need to protect full, free, fair speech. Most experts do not want social media companies or the government to have too much control over what gets said or who gets to speak. The social advocacy group Avaaz has come up with methods to fight disinformation. "We don't say remove content," says Fadi Quran. "We don't say remove pages. Because we do believe in freedom of expression and it can become very dangerous if pages are being removed or deleted."[53] Instead, his group prefers a different tactic. They have urged social media companies to reach out to people who have recently interacted with disinformation and show them a statement explaining that what they saw was not true, along with an explanation and corrected facts.

At Factbook.org, Avaaz shows what Facebook could look like if the company put this suggestion into effect. In a 2020 research study, experts at George Washington University and Ohio State University used this demonstration site to test the impact that

Battling Bots

In order to create a Twitter account, users must be able to verify their contact information and complete a reCAPTCHA test, which usually includes checking a box to confirm "I'm not a robot." The test is very easy for people but very difficult for computer algorithms. If an account has suspicious activity or gets reported by other users, Twitter will throw these sorts of tests at the account again. If it cannot respond quickly enough, it may be suspended. "Eight to 10 million accounts a week are challenged automatically," says Yoel Roth, head of site integrity at Twitter. "More than three-quarters of those accounts wind up removed automatically from the service." That works out to ten to twelve bot accounts getting shut down every second. Despite these efforts, the bots keep on coming. Whenever social media sites create a new rule to attempt to limit bot activity, the people behind the bots find a way around it. For example, if a site sets a rule that accounts get suspended if they post one hundred or more posts per hour, bots will create ninety-nine posts per hour. It is a never-ending battle of measures, countermeasures, and counter-countermeasures.

Quoted in Destin Sandlin, "The Twitter Bot Battle (Who Is Attacking Twitter?)," *Smarter Every Day*, Episode 214, YouTube, April 8, 2019. www.youtube.com/watch?v=V-1RhQ1uuQ4.

corrections could have. They first showed people a typical news feed, then showed them one with corrections added. They found that the corrections decreased belief in the disinformation by an average of 50 percent.

Other research has found that this effect may not last very long. People may forget about a correction after just one week and revert to believing the original information. "The fundamental problem with misinformation is that once people have heard it, they tend to believe and act on it, even after it's been corrected,"[54] says Stephan Lewandowsky, a psychologist at the University of Bristol in the United Kingdom. Researchers are working hard to figure out how to issue corrections in a manner that will stick in people's memories.

Many other experts and independent organizations have come forward with excellent ideas to stem the flow of disinformation, especially on social media. Everyone working on these issues needs public support, government support, and the support of social media organizations. Only then can society make progress toward cleaning up information pollution.

CHAPTER FIVE

Teaching Media Literacy

In January 2019 a group of teenagers and a Native American man had a tense encounter in Washington, DC. The teens were part of a peaceful protest and wore red "Make America Great Again" hats (showing their support for then-president Donald Trump). As the Native American man chanted and beat a drum, one boy stood close and stared at him. A short video clip of this moment went viral on Twitter. The *Washington Post*, CNN, and many other news organizations accused the teens of taunting or harassing the man or blocking his path. The moment sparked outrage, especially among liberals. Covington Catholic, the school that the boys attended, considered expelling them.

However, this video clip did not tell the whole story. It was an example of disinformation. The encounter had actually happened, but important context had been left out. Longer videos revealed that a completely separate group of adult protesters had harassed the teenagers first. The Native American man, who was part of a third group, then walked up directly in front of the boy. The boy said that he had felt "startled and confused"[55] in that moment as he stared at the drumming man. He stood still and did not say anything, hoping that the situation would not get worse. Many had jumped to the conclusion that the boy was a bully, when in fact he was more of a victim. News organizations issued corrections and apologies. "If the Covington Catholic incident was a test, it's one I failed,"[56] confessed Julie Irwin Zimmerman, a journalist at the *Atlantic*.

The Gullible Brain

This story is a perfect example of how disinformation spreads on social media, especially when strong emotions are involved. It is also an example of how polarization pushes people toward different versions of reality. Some liberals claimed the boys were chanting "build the wall"—which was a rallying cry among Trump supporters who wanted stricter border controls. In fact, this slogan was not in the video. Thorough journalism and corrections did eventually reveal the truth. But this did not happen fast enough for the boy and his family and friends, who endured days of abuse and even death threats.

Better standards for social media and for journalism should have prevented the misleading video from spreading so widely. However, human psychology also played a role in this spread. The human brain evolved for survival, not for objectivity. Trusting people who share values and mistrusting outsiders or strangers has typically helped a human community survive. Emotions such as fear or anger also have an important purpose in helping people respond

Disinformation spreads quickly on social media, particularly when strong emotions are involved.

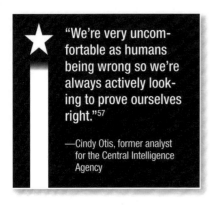

very quickly to threats. All of these important survival instincts, though, make it
more difficult to recognize certain types of
disinformation.

The video of the teenage boy and the
Native American man fooled many people because it seemed to support their
existing stereotypes about how Trump
supporters treat people of color. This is an example of confirma-
tion bias. This bias makes people much more likely to seek out
and believe information that supports views they already have.
People also tend to avoid or ignore information that challenges
their existing views. "We're very uncomfortable as humans being wrong so we're always actively looking to prove ourselves
right,"[57] says Cindy Otis, a former analyst for the Central Intelligence Agency. People are drawn to stories that make their beliefs
and values seem more valid or make them feel like part of a team.
If a story seems like it should be true, and many others already
believe it, most people will just accept it at face value.

The video also triggered people's emotions. In the midst of
anger or fear, people tend to use motivated reasoning. This is
thinking guided by emotions. As a result, "we end up producing
justifications or making decisions based on what outcomes we
want rather than on the actual evidence around us,"[58] says Otis.
The people who liked and shared the video wanted to bring attention to very real and very emotionally fraught issues of racism
in society. However, there was no evidence that this particular
video was actually an example of racist bullying.

Thinking Critically

Though all humans share these biases in belief and behavior, hope
is not lost. The best antidote to bad information and psychological
biases is careful, critical thinking. All individuals have a responsibility
to stay on their toes and think twice about content while browsing
news, especially in today's polluted media environment.

When a person knows how to think critically about content, this is called media literacy. Media literacy is a set of skills that allow people to consume and create media responsibly. They can avoid biases and seek truth and understanding. When exercising these skills, people ask questions like the following: Who made this message and why? What is their point of view? What is the goal of the message? Is the information accurate? What might be missing from this message?

Looking into the original video with media literacy skills would reveal that it is not what it seems. The account that originally posted the clip to Twitter was highly suspicious and later got suspended. It had a name and photo that did not match. It had a high follower count and a very high rate of tweets. A network of anonymous accounts helped boost the video. It likely was not a person exercising his or her right to free speech but a bot spreading discontent.

The CRAAP Test

One important thing to understand about media is that there is much more to a message than what meets the eyes or ears. To thoroughly understand any communication, it is important to

The SHEG Study

In 2018–2019 the Stanford History Education Group (SHEG) had 3,446 students in the US complete six exercises to test their media literacy skills. In the first exercise, they watched a Facebook video that showed people in a room putting ballot after ballot into envelopes. This seemed to show voter fraud. Fifty-two percent of students believed that the video was strong evidence of fraud during the 2016 Democratic primaries in the United States. However, the video had actually been shot in Russia. A quick online search for the video would have revealed that it was disinformation.

In another exercise, students had to consider whether a website about carbon dioxide and science was a reliable source of information. The students were told that they could search online for more information. The few who did discovered that the website was funded by fossil fuel companies, which are motivated to mislead people about climate change. However, 96 percent of students failed to leave the page itself. They were duped by scientific-looking content, the ".org" URL that indicates that it is a nonprofit, and the professional look of the site.

think not just about the content of the message itself but also about the communicator (or author or creator), the medium or channel (Twitter, radio, YouTube, and so on), and the audience. All of these parts of a message help reveal whether it is trustworthy or not.

A great way to check whether a piece of content might be good or bad information is to put it through the CRAAP test. Sarah Blakeslee and a team of librarians at California State University, Chico, first developed this test in 2004. The letters stand for "currency, relevance, authority, accuracy, and purpose." Blakeslee chose letters that spelled out "crap" on purpose. She wanted something that would stick in students' memories. If content fails this test, then it is crap, or worth nothing as information. If it is unclear whether content passes or fails the test, the developers suggest asking a librarian for help. Librarians are trained experts at evaluating information, and it is their job to help match people

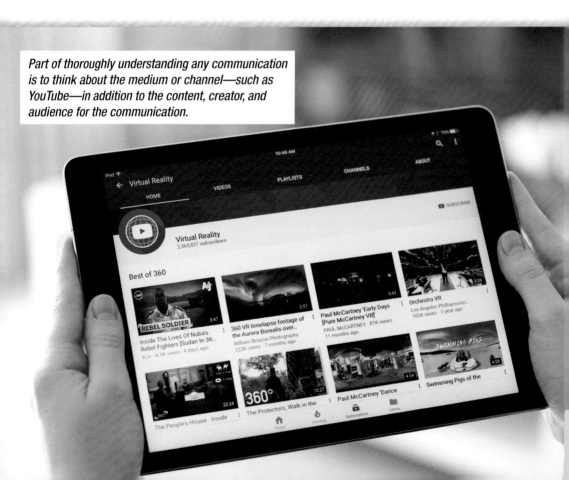

Part of thoroughly understanding any communication is to think about the medium or channel—such as YouTube—in addition to the content, creator, and audience for the communication.

with media of all kinds. Briefly, these are the elements that make up the CRAAP test:

Currency

When was the information published or posted? In general, newer information is more accurate than older information. For example, health experts did not know the best measures to protect against COVID-19 right away. They released new information all the time. Relying on old information could have been unsafe. In some cases historical information is still very useful. Most articles and social media posts are marked with a date, but watch out for reposts or reprints of older information.

Relevance

How important and direct is this information? Persuasive messages often seem very important and urgent when they really are not. Or they may try to distract the audience from understanding complex issues by triggering emotions. Watch out for these tactics. When doing research, make sure to seek out information that is not too basic or too advanced and that directly answers a question.

Authority

Who is the source of the information? Search for the author's name to check if that person actually exists and has the appropriate expertise or credentials to speak with authority. Be wary of authors that hide their identity or are associated with political organizations, companies, or groups that produce propaganda. Online, it may be necessary to trace a piece of content back to an original poster.

Accuracy

Is the information reliable, truthful, and correct? If the information came from a source that is edited and fact-checked, it is usually trustworthy. Examples of reliable news sources include the BBC, the *New York Times*, the *Wall Street Journal*, the *Economist*, the *New Yorker*, the Associated Press, Reuters, Bloomberg News, ProPublica, and more. Also, look for evidence to support the claim, such as a direct quote or a scientific paper or survey. Anecdotes and personal stories add interest but are not great evidence. Images and videos can be excellent evidence, but they may be modified in misleading ways. Check original sources and other reliable sources to see if they agree with the information. Independent fact-checking websites such as Snopes or FactCheck .org can help verify or debunk widespread claims.

Purpose

Why does this information exist? This is a key question to ask. Information that is intended to inform or teach is more reliable than information intended to sell, entertain, persuade, or confuse. If the message is labeled as opinion or advertisement, it likely only contains facts that support the opinion writer's ideas or the advertiser's goals. Most online content is not labeled, but URLs can help. Information from an educational or government institution (.edu or .gov) is typically more reliable than information from a company (.com). Organizations (.org) can go both ways. Read about the authors or institutions behind messages. Do they make their goals and values clear? Do they have any religious, political, cultural, or other biases?

Where Media Literacy Skills Are Lacking

Plenty of resources exist to help children, teens, and adults learn media literacy and practice these skills. Many books, lesson plans, articles, videos, and more are freely available online and in libraries. Unfortunately, these resources do not seem to be reaching as many people as they should. In 2016 the Stanford History Edu-

Plenty of resources are available online to help children, teens, and adults learn media literacy.

cation Group (SHEG) did a study that revealed a severe lack of digital media literacy skills among middle school, high school, and college students. "In every case and at every level, we were taken aback by students' lack of preparation,"[59] the authors wrote. For example, over 80 percent of middle school students believed that a story labeled "sponsored content" was a real news story. In fact, this is a type of advertisement.

In response, many states and institutions came up with ways to try to address the problem. But media literacy has not improved. In 2018 to 2019, SHEG assessed a new set of students. Once again, the students performed terribly. They had to complete six tasks, and 90 percent failed to get any credit on four or more of those tasks. "If we can't find a way to upgrade the skills of ordinary citizens—and fast—democracy itself will be the casualty,"[60] says Sam Wineburg, cofounder of SHEG.

> "If we can't find a way to upgrade the skills of ordinary citizens—and fast—democracy itself will be the casualty."[60]
>
> —Sam Wineburg, cofounder of the Stanford History Education Group

It is not just media literacy skills that are lacking, says Jennifer Kavanagh, a political scientist at the Rand Corporation. People also need science literacy and an understanding of statistics to tell real science and real data from pseudoscience and misleading data. They need an understanding of civics to be able to participate in democracy. Many schools are working hard to make these types of skills a priority. Kavanagh says, "Teachers are really working to integrate this type of material into their classes, but they lack resources. They lack the time, they lack the support, and they lack the actual material."[61] SHEG provides free lessons and assessments for classrooms. But school boards and local governments will have to step up to make sure that teachers and librarians have the time and support they need to add this type of material to their students' already busy schedules.

Coming Together

Media literacy is not just about warding off bad information. Media literacy skills also help a person seek out enjoyable, enlightening, and eye-opening media. People with these skills do not have to exercise them continuously, because they know where to look for information they can trust. Individuals can also use media literacy skills to create media or start conversations that will educate and inform others. They can actively participate in the democratic process.

Media literacy and critical-thinking skills alone will not solve the disinformation crisis. Neither will stronger regulations for social media or more careful and thorough journalism. One of the most important things that everyone will need to do is to come together as a society so we can once again share a common reality. "There is a deep political division in the country . . . and that

Mind the Perception Gap

Most Republicans and Democrats hold much more similar views on controversial issues than most people realize. Dan Vallone calls this a perception gap. For example, 79 percent of Republicans say that racism is still a problem in America. But Democrats think that only half of Republicans would say this. On the opposite side, 85 percent of Democrats disagree with the statement "most police are bad people." Republicans think that only 48 percent would disagree. Vallone estimates that just one-third of Americans hold extreme views. The rest have much more moderate views or are not sure what they think. A perception gap can be dangerous. Vallone's team's report states:

> When Democrats and Republicans believe their opponents hold extreme views, they become more threatened by each other. They start seeing each other as enemies, and start believing they need to win at all costs. They make excuses for their own side cheating and breaking the rules to beat the other side. . . . This is how countries fall into a cycle of deepening polarization, and how democracies die.

Daniel Yudkin et al., *The Perception Gap: How False Impressions Are Pulling Americans Apart*. New York: More in Common, 2019. https://perceptiongap.us.

has been worsening over time,"[62] says Dan Vallone, US director at More in Common, an organization that researches polarization and develops strategies for how to counter it.

The situation is not as terrible as the media and some politicians make it seem. Most Americans do not hold radical or extreme views. Most have inconsistent views or do not engage much with politics. So how can Americans stop distrusting each other? Vallone suggests "fostering more intellectual curiosity and empathy."[63] That includes having conversations with people who hold different viewpoints. "We have to begin to talk to one other again," says Lee C. McIntyre. "We have to not just accept the fact that our society is polarized and fragmented. . . . As individuals, we can start to listen to one another again . . . to not shy away from hard conversations."[64]

The real voices of all Americans and all citizens of the world matter. If people can find a way to speak their truths and also hear others' truths, while filtering out or ignoring information pollution, then there will be hope for freedom and democracy.

SOURCE NOTES

Introduction: An Attack on the Government

1. Quoted in Dmitriy Khavin et al., "Day of Rage: How Trump Supporters Took the U.S. Capitol," *New York Times*, June 30, 2021. www.nytimes.com.
2. Quoted in Robert Moore, "Donald Trump Agrees to Leave White House Once Result Is Certified," ITV News, November 27, 2020. www.itv.com.
3. Quoted in Brennan Center for Justice, "It's Official: The Election Was Secure," December 11, 2020. www.brennancenter.org.
4. Quoted in Brennan Center for Justice, "It's Official."
5. Quoted in Juana Summers, "Congress Certifies Biden Victory; Trump Pledges 'Orderly Transition' on Jan. 20," NPR, January 7, 2021. www.npr.org.
6. Quoted in Quote Investigator, "A Lie Can Travel Halfway Around the World While the Truth Is Putting On Its Shoes," 2014. https://quoteinvestigator.com.

Chapter One: Good Information Matters

7. Quoted in Greg Sukiennik, "Manchester Students Rally Against Single-Use Plastic Bags," *Bennington (VT) Banner*, October 4, 2018. www.benningtonbanner.com.
8. Laura Neuman, "A Key to Democracy: Access to Information Critical for Citizens, Governments," Carter Center, April 11, 2005. www.cartercenter.org.
9. Quoted in Mike Hind, "Fighting for Truth in a Post–Fake News World—Interviews from Misinfocon," November 15, 2017, in *The Disinformation Age*, podcast. https://uk-podcasts.co.uk.
10. First Draft, "About," 2021. https://firstdraftnews.org/about.
11. Quoted in Hind, "Fighting for Truth in a Post–Fake News World—Interviews from Misinfocon."
12. Quoted in David Hawkings, "Far-Right Trump Fan Faces Rare Criminal Charge for '16 Social Media Vote Scam," Fulcrum, January 28, 2021. https://thefulcrum.us.
13. Donald J. Trump, *Break In*, YouTube, July 20, 2020. www.youtube.com/watch?v=moZOrq0qL3Q.

Chapter Two: Tap, Like, Share

14. Quoted in Jenna Spinelle, "How Conspiracies Are Damaging Democracy," September 1, 2019, in *Democracy Works*, podcast. www.npr.org.
15. Philip Montgomery, "Get Up, Stand Up," *Wired*, November 2015. www.wired.com.
16. Samuel Woolley, *The Reality Game: How the Next Wave of Technology Will Break the Truth*. New York: Hachette, 2020, p. 3.
17. Woolley, *The Reality Game*, p. 9.
18. Quoted in Callum Borchers, "Twitter Executive on Fake News: 'We Are Not the Arbiters of Truth,'" *Washington Post*, February 8, 2018. www.washingtonpost.com.
19. Quoted in Tom McCarthy, "Zuckerberg Says Facebook Won't Be 'Arbiters of Truth' After Trump Threat," *The Guardian* (Manchester, UK), May 28, 2020. www.theguardian.com.
20. Jonah Berger, "Want Your Ad to Go Viral? Activate These Emotions," *Harvard Business Review*, February 4, 2021. https://hbr.org.
21. Quoted in Amanda Seitz and Hannah Fingerhut, "Americans Agree Misinformation Is a Problem, Poll Shows," AP, October 8, 2021. https://apnews.com.
22. Quoted in Peter Dizikes, "Study: On Twitter, False News Travels Faster than True Stories," MIT News, March 8, 2018. https://news .mit.edu.
23. Quoted in Dizikes, "Study."
24. Quoted in Anne Applebaum, "Fake News Is Solvable," July 10, 2019, in *Solvable*, podcast. https://podcasts.apple.com.
25. Quoted in Kelsey Munro, "Panel Discussion: The Disinformation Age—Can Democracy Survive Social Media?," Lowy Institute, November 27, 2019, podcast. www.lowyinstitute.org.
26. Woolley, *The Reality Game*, p. 38.

Chapter Three: A Post-Truth World

27. Quoted in Hind, "Fighting for Truth in a Post–Fake News World—Interviews from Misinfocon."
28. Quoted in Mila Atmos, "Post-Truth: Lee C. McIntyre," May 14, 2020, in *Future Hindsight*, podcast. www.futurehindsight.com.
29. Matt Taibbi. *Hate Inc: Why Today's Media Makes Us Despise One Another*. New York: OR Books, 2019.
30. Quoted in Yuen Yiu, "Visualizing Twitter Echo Chambers," Inside Science, March 18, 2020. www.insidescience.org.

31. Quoted in William Cummings, "'Alternative Facts' to 'Witch Hunt': A Glossary of Trump Terms," *USA Today*, January 16, 2018. www.usatoday.com.
32. Quoted in John Haltiwanger, "Republicans Have Built a Cult of Personality Around Trump That Glosses Over His Disgraced Presidency," Business Insider, March 4, 2021. www.businessinsider.com.
33. Quoted in Janna Anderson and Lee Rainie, "The Future of Truth and Misinformation Online," Pew Research Center, October 19, 2017. www.pewresearch.org.
34. Quoted in Brett Samuels, "Trump Ramps Up Rhetoric on Media, Calls Press 'the Enemy of the People,'" *The Hill* (Washington, DC), April 5, 2019. https://thehill.com.
35. Quoted in Tracy Staedter, "Neil deGrasse Tyson Warns Science Denial Could 'Dismantle' Democracy," Live Science, April 20, 2017. www.livescience.com.
36. Quoted in Spinelle, "How Conspiracies Are Damaging Democracy."
37. Quoted in Atmos, "Post-Truth."
38. Quoted in Anil Dash, "Stopping Fake News," November 27, 2019, in *Function with Anil Dash*, podcast. https://podcasts.voxmedia.com.
39. Quoted in Munro, "Panel Discussion."
40. Quoted in Munro, "Panel Discussion."

Chapter Four: Stopping the Lies

41. Society of Professional Journalists, "SPJ Code of Ethics," September 6, 2014. www.spj.org.
42. Quoted in Darragh Worland, "Who Are Journalism's New Gatekeepers?," October 21, 2020, in *Is That a Fact?*, podcast. https://newslit.org.
43. Quoted in Darragh Worland, "How Can the Press Serve Our Fractured Country?," October 21, 2020, in *Is That a Fact?*, podcast. https://newslit.org.
44. Quoted in Munro, "Panel Discussion."
45. Colin Crowell, "Our Approach to Bots and Misinformation," *Company* (blog), Twitter, June 14, 2017. https://blog.twitter.com.
46. Quoted in Niamh McIntyre, "Group That Spread False Covid Claims Doubled Facebook Interactions in Six Months," *The Guardian* (Manchester, UK), October 21, 2021. www.theguardian.com.
47. Quoted in ANC News, *White House: Facebook Not Doing Enough to Stop Spread of COVID-19 Misinformation*, YouTube, July 16, 2021. www.youtube.com/watch?v=oq6Yl9Mrv6U.
48. Quoted in Karen Hao, "How Facebook Got Addicted to Spreading Misinformation," *MIT Technology Review*, March 11, 2021. www.technologyreview.com.

49. Nancy Watzman, "How Political Ad Transparency Can Help Fix Democracy's Cybersecurity Problem," Democracy Fund, August 7, 2020. https://democracyfund.org.
50. Quoted in Chris Fox, "Social Media: How Might It Be Regulated?," BBC, November 12, 2020. www.bbc.com.
51. Quoted in Applebaum, "Fake News Is Solvable."
52. Chris Tenove et al., "Poisoning Democracy: How Canada Can Address Harmful Speech Online," Public Policy Forum, November 8, 2018. https://ppforum.ca.
53. Quoted in Dash, "Stopping Fake News."
54. Quoted in Zara Abrams, "Controlling the Spread of Misinformation," American Psychological Association, March 1, 2021. www.apa.org.

Chapter Five: Teaching Media Literacy

55. Quoted in Editorial Board, "MAGA-Hatted Teens, a Native American and the Peril of Instant Judgment," *Chicago Tribune*, January 21, 2019. www.chicagotribune.com.
56. Julie Irwin Zimmerman, "I Failed the Covington Catholic Test," *The Atlantic*, January 21, 2019. www.theatlantic.com.
57. Quoted in Darragh Worland, "The Mainstreaming of Conspiracy Theories," November 2, 2020, in *Is That a Fact?*, podcast. https://newslit.org.
58. Quoted in Worland, "The Mainstreaming of Conspiracy Theories."
59. Stanford History Education Group, "Evaluation Information: The Cornerstone of Civic Online Reasoning," November 22, 2016. https://stacks.stanford.edu.
60. Quoted in Carrie Spector, "As the 2020 Election Approaches, Stanford Scholars Teach Skills to Judge Fact from Fiction Online," Stanford News, October 7, 2020. https://news.stanford.edu.
61. Quoted in Darragh Worland, "Truth Decay: Why Americans Are Turning Away from Facts," November 11, 2020, in *Is That a Fact?*, podcast. https://newslit.org.
62. Quoted in Darragh Worland, "Perception or Reality: Just How Divided Is America, Really?," October 14, 2020, in *Is That a Fact?*, podcast. https://newslit.org.
63. Quoted in Worland, "Perception or Reality."
64. Quoted in Atmos, "Post-Truth."

Books

Kathryn Hulick, *Thinking Critically: Fake News*. San Diego, CA: ReferencePoint, 2020.

Michelle Luhtala and Jacquelyn Whiting, *News Literacy: The Keys to Combating Fake News*. Santa Barbara, CA: Libraries Unlimited, 2018.

Michael Miller, *Fake News: Separating Truth from Fiction*. Minneapolis, MN: Twenty-First Century, 2019.

Barbara Sheen, *The Fake News Crisis: How Misinformation Harms Society*. San Diego, CA: ReferencePoint, 2022.

Samuel Woolley, *The Reality Game: How the Next Wave of Technology Will Break the Truth*. New York: Hachette, 2020.

Internet Sources

Janna Anderson and Lee Rainie, "Many Tech Experts Say Digital Disruption Will Hurt Democracy," Pew Research Center, February 21, 2020. www.pewresearch.org.

Megan Brenan, "Americans Remain Distrustful of Mass Media," Gallup, September 30, 2020. https://news.gallup.com.

Anil Dash, "Stopping Fake News," November 27, 2019, in *Function with Anil Dash*, podcast. https://podcasts.voxmedia.com.

Kelsey Munro, "Panel Discussion: The Disinformation Age—Can Democracy Survive Social Media?," Lowy Institute, November 27, 2019, podcast. www.lowyinstitute.org.

Jenna Spinelle, "How Conspiracies Are Damaging Democracy," September 1, 2019, in *Democracy Works*, podcast. www.npr.org.

Organizations and Websites

Brookings Institution
www.brookings.edu
This think tank conducts research aimed at solving problems in society. Research areas include foreign policy, economics, development, governance, and disinformation.

Kettering Foundation

www.kettering.org

This nonprofit organization conducts research exploring the question of what it takes to make democracy work as it should. This research especially focuses on how people can work together to address problems such as disinformation.

More in Common

www.moreincommon.com

This international organization works to confront the polarization threatening democracies in the United States, United Kingdom, France, and Germany.

National Association for Media Literacy Education

https://namle.net

The goal of this organization is to promote media literacy as an essential life skill and help teach people the critical-thinking and communication skills they need in order to be active, thoughtful citizens.

News Literacy Project

https://newslit.org

This organization offers programs that teach students the skills they need to become smart news consumers and active participants in democracy. Its ongoing podcast *Is That a Fact?* is an especially helpful source for understanding disinformation.

Stanford History Education Group

https://sheg.stanford.edu

This organization seeks to improve education by providing materials young people and their educators can use to evaluate online content.

INDEX

$32.95